MW01612191

Mind Composition
In Verse

A Collection of Poems

MIND COMPOSITION

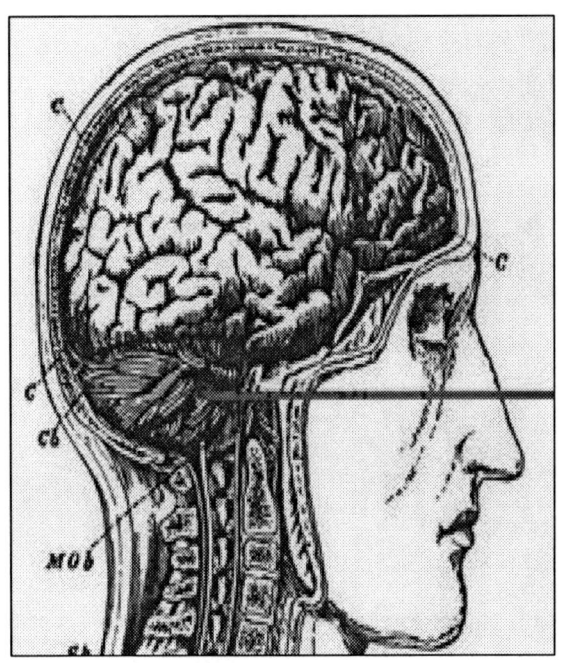

IN VERSE
A Collection of Poems

By
Terrance B. McGee

E-BookTime, LLC
Montgomery, Alabama

Mind Composition in Verse
A Collection of Poems

Copyright © 2005 by Terrance B. McGee

All rights reserved. No part of this book may be reproduced or transmitted in any form or by any means, electronic or mechanical, including photocopying, recording, or by any information storage and retrieval system, without permission in writing from the copyright owner.

ISBN: 978-1-59824-454-0

First Edition
Published February 2007
E-BookTime, LLC
6598 Pumpkin Road
Montgomery, AL 36108
www.e-booktime.com

Acknowledgements

This book is dedicated
In loving memory of my Grandparents:

Fraigia and Lucy McGee

Also,

to my wonderful Mom Dianne, for always considering me your "Miracle Child," Uncle Michael, who has been like a father to me throughout my years; Aunt Lucy and Aunt Sandra, who has been like a second mother to me; Uncle Friagia, Dale, aunt Debra, and Aunt Anne, you four have always provided tremendous support to me in times of need; My Brother Michael and Warren, you two are my blood line towards a successful journey; My Sister Precious, you are definitely that and truly my sweetheart; My wonderful Cousins: Glenda, Reggie, Sonja, Ashley, Jeffrey, Shara, Cassandra, Mikayla, and Kansera, thanks for always believing in me and being that of encouragement; My true friends Lawrence Cedric Pride and Orien Jabe' Thompson, thanks for inspiring me to continue my passion to write; Last but not least, to my magnificent wife LaTisha and my two lovely daughters, Myra and Dominike, you three are truly my Bread & Butter; You are the heart and soul of my many accomplishments. Thanks for being more than supportive of me and also my number one fans; without you, I'd have no drive and nothing to strive for. I love you all tremendously, with all my heart.

Contents

Contents

From the very day life began to the day I was conceived, there is a great fact that lies within; time is that fact. Everyday which goes by, every year, every century, the necessity to agree with that, that which is real, develops my senses to adjust and conform so that I may survive. Every tick, every second that goes by is honored in the same manner, I breathe the air around me. Without time I would not be who I am today. In fact, I may not have been here at all. I exist, therefore I am. I am a Poet. I wish to present to you my own writing, which will explain why I have chosen time to best describe my life and myself as how it applies to my existence.

Time

A rhythm measure of duration

My leisure to cope within my own existence

I become obsessed within my own dimensions

Suppressing a timepiece to maintain a leveled balance

Coincide, while I engage to what is formally known as Time

Traversing around as the earth continues to spin

Reversed future back an hour

I was late because the battery in my watch stopped

Royal acts of dependency

Lost without hope I become confused

Life being not useful without seconds, minutes that makes up an hour

Revolved mind, thoughts crawling across the globe

Remaining unsure of the savings time

At first hot then cold, it being dark the whole moment

In retrospect, not knowing time I'd know not where I'd be

Every since the day of birth, life has been a struggle for me. I recall my mother telling me that I almost didn't make it. She also said that I was very sick and didn't eat at all for weeks. She told me how the hospital kept me and continued to diagnose me. I don't recall any of it, but what I do realize, is why she'd always consider me her miracle child. Still to this day, I often wonder if that was the case, I looked death in the eyes and didn't know if I'd make it. Whenever I felt that my times were so difficult, I'd always remember someone has it worse than me.

Life

The most beautiful part of life is to live

I've witness a close death

It was dark and it was frightening

Black suits, black dresses and black shoes

Tears around the casket

Fortunate to breathe one breathe at a time

How vital is your life to you?

Are you so sure that you'll see the next day?

First you're here, then decayed

Understand the position that you hold

God has grant you this moment

Use it wisely to make a change

Everyone lose in the mystery of life

Self-study shows that everyone must perish someday

While continuation of the heart rise and fall

No matter the situation, give thanks that you live

From the time that I've been capable of writing, I've had a joy collaborating thoughts, while placing them on paper. Whether it was drawing little stick men and women, cartoon characters, or simply the Bart Simpson configurations. I understood that it was very much a hobby, only during that time, I didn't realize the writing values worth. Writing has always been my way of expression; Therefore, I've painted a mental picture which describes my way of thinking.

Poet

I'm a Poet, which is what I am

My mind manifest into a systematic universe

Whereas, I'm gone off into a deep cosmos

Imaginary thoughts are invented

Revealing a discover about the facts of life

So profound it may sound, sparking everyone's interest

My urge is to meet people's appetite

With ideas through expressions that are real

The various concepts may even sound unique

In actuality, it is a destiny, or a formal experience

I'm a Poet, which is what I am

My reputation is a form of anticipation with perception

To understand a thought and make wise decisions

It's a gift of nature to foresee a destiny

Through my writings, showing insight to acknowledge consequences

Through perception, I understand people and their various outcomes

Through visualization, I'm only a Poet

That is what I am

Before proposing some words of wisdom to you, allow me to say, there's a message to be heard in every poem. In the world today many people of various cities, states, and countries experience trying times, whether they are good, bad, happy or sad. I hope that you enjoy this collaboration of art and perhaps find interesting those, which apply to you.

Writers Anthem

As I read to you these words that are written

The nation waits patiently

Suspense minds of curiosity

Not a sound in the world

Quiet; everyone listens

There is one sound, that which I speak

I propose these words of wisdom with glare

Surrendering the facts of truth to be known

This forecast of anticipation is a prospect to come

Lending your ears in advance to hear such profound realization

Some sayings will make you cry, some will make you laugh

Some will intensify your thoughts reminiscing your past

Some sayings will teach you things, some will make you glow

Some will energize your mood from a procrastinated hold

Some sayings are confessions; some will lift your soul

Some will bring to your attention, all this time you've been wrong

Some sayings you will like; some you will not

Some will act as reminders just in case you forgot

I pledge allegiance to the people that my writing won't stop

Engraved on paper, signed …the writers block

At the age of five, not only did I have an interest for writing and drawing, but also playing sports. As time progressed, I'd become pretty talented in several sports. There was one sport that I so loved the most; Basketball. Over the years I became the most valuable player on the court, and it started in my very own backyard. I am grateful to have had an uncle who cared so dearly about me; possessed much of his valuable time just so I'd succeed. I've utilized my potential, played ball in various places, giving thanks to all those who've always supported me.

Basketball

I skinned my knee playing basketball

Mama rubs with alcohol

Said, "Boy get back on the court"

Tough guy I was

Uncle taught me the game

Tall… stood a bought six feet four

Everyone was scared to guard him

Dribbling with force towards the rim

Same rim from my bicycle

Yet, I had no shame

My backyard was full of people

Starting from roosters when they crow

Grandpa said, "It was time to come in"

Maybe this'll be my favorite sport

Tomorrow do the same thing over again

As a young man I learned a lot from my Grandfather. He taught me
to be wise, independent, and to work for what I wanted. I was
fortunate of that, never lazy, but eager to earn a buck. I use to work
during the summer, mowed lawns, picked bottles and cans. I had
expensive taste for the latest fashion; therefore, I knew something
must give. Every year before school started, just as many students, I
wanted to show off my new threads. A desperate young man,
worked hard as a teen.

Brand New

Hey! I paid for those jeans

                                        I've earned myself one hundred dollars

                         How much for that hat?

I still have seventy dollars

                                            My favorite shirt

                      That'll make me broke

The same old clothes

                                            But I need new ones

                     I work this whole summer

Lazy people don't get paid

                                      Those shoes fit me good

                    Mother disagrees

Those socks must cost a lot

                                       So I try them on

                Brown is my favorite color

That belt is just my size

                            I carry my wallet with me

                Now I have nothing in it

All because I bought everything brand new

As a young man, I've always had a head full of hair. In fact, I was born with a head full of hair. My mother kept pictures so I'd see just how long my hair had grown. She'd braid it up for me, seeing it hang down to my shoulders. My Grandfather felt it'd be wise to get it cut, so he'd take me with him down to see his old barber. Waiting my turn, I listen to the guys joke about whose hair was the toughest. Everyone was laughing; it was quite a hilarious moment.

Nappy Hair

Deeply rooted

Existing an abundance of filaments from my skin

No artificial

Every string lacking any succulent herb

Very sensitive and course

I experience such great deal of pain

In lack thereof, because I seldom try to utilize a comb

Resembling wool

I'm convinced that this makes me so natural

Being proud of me and mine

Excepting the fact, I have "Nappy Hair"

I grew up in a very small town, not quite the type of place that inspires an individual hopes and dreams. Trying to be that good citizen, I watch men and women around me destroy and ruin their lives. It never rendered in my mind to be that way, but instead provided motivation to become successful and productive. All the time I'd wish for bigger and better things, surrounded by drug affiliation, seeing people dreams fade away. Somehow someday; hopefully, things would change.

Bucket of Blood

Leave me be, I'd much rather be alone

Says an old man without a care in the world

Around the old block where Mr. Massacre reside

The formally known psychiatrist neighborhood street pharmacist

Allow me to let go of my frustration and extract my thoughts

To a place of impatience where I'm illegally blind folded

The grass here grows in many different types of weed

A very fortunate spot… did I mention that I smoke?

I once had a job, now it seems I stay broke

Sick to my stomach … remembering, I have yet to eat

Loosing much weight and also feeling blown away

Somehow someway, I have to get some spare change

Around the corner is where I live

Spent most of time around the corner

Out of my home and on the streets

I now reside at the Bucket of Blood

Life can be so devastating at times; the idea is to overcome such tragedy with isolation from a depressive state of mind. My Grandparents adopted me at such young age because my mother felt it was the right thing to do. Always missing a part of me, trying to find that missing piece, things weren't the same without my dad and mother being around. That split moment of release seems to have taken a part of me, yet; things happen for a reason.

Riot

There is a Riot going on

Are you fighting back?

There is a Riot going on

Whose side are you on?

There is a Riot going on

I never had a dad to teach me the political side of things

There is a riot going on

Mother wasn't able to sustain the fight with me

So hey! Meet my new mom

There is a Riot going on

Compliments of the struggle, I'm able to sustain more than the average man

There is a Riot going on

Who really cares about what goes on in other countries?

There is a Riot going on

Consisting of reality and facts

There is a Riot going on

Look! My brother is fighting too

There is a Riot going on

Between aids and drugs, we're losing that war

There is a Riot going on

Who's left to fight?

If I had known while I was younger, I would have been more inspiring

Maybe I'd still have many of my people alive today.

I can recall that time in school when I first start caring about the opposite sex. More like a crush, without that person actually knowing. I use to write love notes, too shy to give it to her myself; instead, I would send it by friend or associate. We all have experienced at one point in our lives, sharing feelings and thoughts for someone who we hardly even knew.

Secret Admirer

Scarlet red tone,

Your intervene my mood of distress with a welcoming chance of temptation love

Diamond eyes, shining, glittering

Controlling the wind, you move so swift

One leg at a time, left before the right

You're the boundary line of my space, my circle, and my thoughts

Did I mention my thoughts?

You're the supreme highlight and permanent element that override my frustration

Didn't you notice I exist now with a glow?

I know who you are; you're the sophisticated one

Smell good, look good, simply an appetizer

I know what you eat; where you live, and what you like

I'm no stalker; only a Secret Admirer

Sometimes in life while wanting something so badly, you'd do almost anything just to get it. I hadn't achieved much from being a Secret Admirer, but knew definitely, this particular girl was truly the one. Majority of my precious thoughts were consumed by fantasizing about her, whether she sees me the way I foresee her, in my mind she'd always be the one.

Mystery Lady

Her eyes seem so relaxed

Meditating with a delicate stare

At ease was her mind

Marked by minute precision as she contemplate

Her ways were divine

Her intellect spoke with a sense of inspiration

Ultimately so desirable, with no expectancy

Just fatal beauty carrying out the ways of enigma

A desired taste what appeared she had

Acquiring those characteristics of lady like tactics

Her soft voice comparative to that of a feather

She was too astonishing to approach

If given the chance, I'll just treat her exclusive

She will always remain my mystery lady

I grew up in the church when I was younger.
Mother would always ensure that I was up, looking good, and ready to go. As time moved on, seem I had gotten away from my old Christian boy image. Unknowingly, I was just more interested with living that old teenage lifestyle. Just as the average teenager in high school, I was eager to try different things, as if I had something to prove. As time pressed on, the importance of school became more challenging, this in term possessed me to soul search and become wiser.

Why Shouldn't I be in One

I was standing alone one day, while acknowledging Gods
wonderful creation

All of a sudden without being hesitant crosses my mind the thought
of salvation

As if it was a dream joyful noises filled the air

Giving me such great feeling that was appointing me out somewhere

Filled with suspense, asking myself what could it be?

Along come this Christian guy that began talking to me

I close my eyes and begin to cry, ashamed of the way I had lived

He told me stories of the Almighty one, which had changed the way
that I felt

Now I began to realize what such melodies meant to me

It was God Himself awakening me, allowing the sight of reality

He introduced me to a nearby church where they praise and worship
Him

I ask forgiveness of all my sins although they were caught on film

Advice to lost souls that feel so blue, you could do the same

Give your life to a merciful God it's a privilege to know His name

I myself wish for eternal life though my work for Him is never done

There are various church to choose from so why shouldn't I be in one?

I've reached that point in my life of wondering about love. I wasn't sure what it was, but I was eager to find out. I was willing to give my heart to that one special person. I just wasn't sure if she wanted to be with me. I'm not talking marriage, but with every relationship there has got to be a starting point.

Desperate Desire

Sitting quietly, contemplating as the mind drifts off into outer space

Having this thirst for love, more than anything ever held in your possession

Desperate emotions wait to burst from within

Feeling being kept secret, forms a burning desire

You have allusions, as imaginary thoughts make the temperature rise

Visualize beautiful sketch in disguise

Still waiting to exhale

Become overwhelmed from being caressed by even the slightest touch

Loose total control

Emotions run wild, from such passionate thrill

All thoughts are put on hold, dangerous it gets when making assumptions

Never rush possibilities; love can hurt worse than anything

I guess I've learned one thing about rushing into love, you can't find love; it just finds you. Although I sense what it takes to love someone, I was capable of recognizing a dishonest heart. You could never make someone love you, but you could always love that individual, disregarding how they feel about you. I had a kind and generous heart, but was stunt by surprise.

My X

You had crippled my heart temporary

Dishonest you were, cruel and so silly

I cried for you because I was young and immature

Seeking desire, possessing unusual stimulations

Like my grandfather, I was taught to be wise

The truth I'd recognized that you didn't care for me

A phantom you were, disappeared from my life

Withheld in mind, you only live in my past

I know now how to read a treacherous heart

Guilty looks hand crafted, written all over the face

The moment of truth as it appears before light

Blunt and so cold you tried to keep the truth concealed

I've learned from mistakes today living a different life

Used a marker which was permanent

Crossed you out as being My X

It was once said, "Never let love keep you down." That's easy to say when you didn't put your all into it. I was strong-minded; besides, had more important things in life to worry about. With a great deal of Faith, I was able to start over from the beginning.

Recovery

The end of a new beginning for the rest of my days

Distress of a black heart, my soul has been placed on ice

No remorse, no rejoice

The back of my mind carries those thoughts

Returning to my life, being not trapped in a dark hole of self-pity

The game of life I use to play

Now the end of a new beginning for the rest of my days

I was caught but fault my way through this ordeal

Is this real, am I experiencing that self-resolution?

Case and point, I now draw my conclusion...

I've recovered

Time has really flown, years ago; I use to wonder what it was like to be out and on my own. Well, let's just say that everything was happening faster than I expected. Tenth grade now, time were approaching to make the biggest decision of all time; what to do after graduating high school. Skilled and multi-talented; yet, I had no clue.

ConFUsiON

I

Am   very   confused

At   This

Point   In   My

Life

I grew up in a small rural town in the Delta. My school had been separated amongst those of different race. I wasn't taught to be prejudice, but knew one day that I was soon face it. There were trying times and misunderstandings. I'm a firm believer that when you learn better you do better. Disregarding the misconception of how I was seen, I was the better person to realize some people just didn't understand.

Stereotype

Perception is assault within the mind of imagination

Dead I tell you

A black soul placed on ice if an objection of knowledge

A disappearing act of all rights

Unhinged consequences, if not formulated in term of apology

Being truly sorry

Judge no other for what one does not understand

Scorching depression, a raging fire

Abandoned self-knowing nothing but to run away being ignorant

Shame is a bit of concern

I lecture you about the truth

Now it all starts to make sense

I ask your forgiveness if I was wrong

Finally, I'm that much closer to becoming a senior in high school. I'm now in the eleventh grade; things are more frightening then before, while the time was still spinning. What's next? Here I go thinking I could choose love again. Infatuated approach, this time love had patience, I was yet to know her true feelings about me.

Intoxicated

I've surrendered my heart to the best thing since slice bread

Every slice so vital

Meaning more to me than any supernaculum Brandy

Scratching my cranium, even the tongue remain speechless

Sensitive to sound, finding a way to spill those three letter words

Knowing my world is revolved around her existence

To have it all

I'd drown first to provide what's vital for her keepsake

Runny eyes and nose

Her can of oil slippery like that of hair grease

Losing my balance

I'd have what she's drinking

Idiot drunk intoxicated

Hoping to be within the same circumference as she

Sensual in mind

Indulging to the highest degree of thoughts about her

Waiting to be pinched

Unless the love she too feel is genuine about me

I appreciate love when it is true, I'd become more alive because I had a clearer view. Love has its hand out with acceptance for keep, I never agreed to everything, but this girl chose me. I'd become her vital factor with feelings I owed her something.

Thievery Beauty

I'm infatuated of such beauty

Gorgeous is how you appear to me

Perfect and so desirable

Thoughts of you that seems unbelievable

You've captured my heart in an unusual way

Now it's always vital to do the things that are small and essential

You are quite a defined work of art

How grateful am I to call you mine

This is why it's never difficult, but so easy to love you

Comfort is what you bring me

You make my life joyful and fantastic

You're more than the other half of me

You're that better half that complete me and make me whole

You enlighten me with only your smile

You leave me stranded in desire

Yes desire, that amusement that's hot like fire

Your presence no dream it's legitimate

For I know that the Lord is real

Although I hate the ways of a person that steals

I love the thief which has stolen my heart

Twelfth grade now, I've become a senior. What will I do next; still discombobulated? I spent much of my time trying to hang with some friends, skipped school doing what I wanted to. I was losing focus, forgetting about the bigger picture, I just couldn't explain what had gotten into me. Sometimes there were no explanations why anything would happen.

On Escape from Reality

Horrible days and terrible nights

Exists a catastrophe when disaster strikes

Strange dreams of lost souls such a terrible waste

Scary thoughts intervene a shortage of time at such fast pace

My future lay ahead for I'm alive but not awake

I see shadows of my fears holding photos of options I could take

I'm terrified of my adversaries, for whom shall I trust

Money is the rule of evil that's apparently not enough

My actions are taken for granted though I seem to do nothing right

It comes to a conclusion, a phase that I myself must fight

I try sacrificing for what is a right, still life tragedy seem contrary

If patience is the key, what's the reason for tales told by a fairy?

As I cruise throughout life difficulties, with low self-esteem, I have frustration

Should I get some counseling, or need motivation?

Any choice except incarceration

After reading these words does it boost your morale, or does it not mean a thing?

You could be that someone who's procrastinating

On escape from living your dreams

Before graduating high school, my grandparents are now deceased, that was very nerve wrecking but my sweetheart stood right by my side. She is my Angel to be and understood most of what I've had to deal with. With love soaked kisses, she'd make me smile again. Loving her being and her existence; she'd be the perfect one for me.

Ideal lady

Come as you are my sweet Angel

Being you're so natural and pure

Comparative you are not

Seems there is no other quite like you

You are God's gift placed on earth

Making my life a magnificent one

Still I'm under the impression, the Lord took more time while
perfecting you

Your eyes has a glare that paces my heartbeat

Your smile encourage my worries with pure satisfaction

I have an announcement to all women of the world

No hard feelings, but my baby is the best in the world

Gorgeous, oh she's more than that

Sporting her stylist wear and having her hair groomed

I'm inspired by her sense of intellect

Her understanding and compromising help to love her even more

Sweetheart, just because you should know

You truly are… my "Ideal lady"

After high school, I remained indecisive with conclusion. I didn't accept scholarships being offered by numerous colleges. It wasn't uncommon to take a break, or at least that's how I felt. Being not useful to life's opportunities can ruin one's self esteem and promote false desire to ever accomplishing a dream. I had become vegetated and nauseated to self worth.

My Self Esteem

What dreams may come as the time never stops?

Just yesterday a thought, then the millennium appeared

In denial of letting time slip me by

Without reasons to procrastinate, I'm left lonely and
unaccompanied

Poor excuses and explanations sound so very tiring

Working hard to be a make belief, it even upsets the dead

"My future lies ahead," for I've heard that before

Time after time I've tripped and fallen; over my own shoe strings

Guilt imbedded within me

My self-esteem has gone down the drain

Hurt me ole mind in the head where it aches

For this pain, no aspirin will ever work

The road I've traveled no one seem to have followed

Maybe they see burden tracks I leave lying ahead

Do not cry ole eyes you may flood the town

Without limitations, you could cry up a sea

Poor legs get back up you can't quit just yet

Keep walking on by trying; there's always hope tomorrow

My love and I had become separated; spread thin across the state, but I lost no care, I lost trust in the relationship worth. How much of a fool had I been? My whole desire had let go and all that's left was memory. I had reached a point in my life when the chances became slim but not so much a defeat. I challenged my own senses to overcome what needed to be done.

Headspace & Timing

I'm in need of Christ therapy

I've been hypnotized to the ways of society

It's dark in my life

To take risk seem to be my only light

To even think escape

I'm tired of dreaming that I've made it out the hood

All I know is that I'm trapped

Constantly fighting to sustain life miseries

Personally, to be someone who love listening to music

I'm also tired of bobbing my head to the same old sad songs

Being me, what do I gain from it?

Earthly judgments and stereotypes

I'll probably be looked upon as being too different

Possibly, considered abnormal

Who am I?

I'm really not sure

Along with the tragedies I'm experiencing

Is it not too late to override such tragedies?

Maybe make some changes in these days of time

Some say I shine, but I don't feel like a star

I have many expectations, but will I meet any of them?

I'm not an alcoholic or consume alcoholic beverages

A many times I feel intoxicated

Simple fact, my life goes through cycles

I suppose to have standards one must first have capabilities

I can see how I want to live not knowing the steps it takes to get there

From days to weeks, from weeks to months, from months to years

It has to be true time does pass at the speed of light

I spend majority of my precious time just thinking

How much time is there left to think?

With all confusion that frustrates me from making wise decisions

It comes to my conclusion, I lack… Headspace & timing

A structured mind thinking grown, I became overwhelmed to nonessentials that meant truly nothing to me. I was losing opportunities from start, and my pieces to the puzzle; I had yet, the perfect match yet.

The Young & Restless

Confined to the ways of society

Lost without hope, I shall not waste my time anymore

A depressed mentality keeps me hating myself

For some things I shall never understand

I enjoy being me, but suffer consequences of the outcome

I am but a magnet-claiming innocent instead

In my eyes I'm trapped with no escape

Nothing ever makes sense, having your cake and eating it too

I hide behind my pride keeping the truth of me concealed

While looking in the mirror only reflects my inner side

Fictitious thoughts exist from a hallucinated mind

The aftermath that causes sorrow if left imbedded in me

Artifacts from past sources, I must let go and leave behind

My future I would never see unless my heart and mind has been set
free

Just as the leaves from the trees that turn brown in the fall

I was that colorful leaf before there was a temperature change

To be an ideal man of his word

I feel that my wisdom is stronger than pride

And my maturity would keep me standing strong

I'd be a fool to let life chances slip me by, I was never raised like this, in fact; I should be ashamed. It doesn't feel so good being at the bottom of the pit. Somehow someway, I must reunite with God. For He that believes, all things are possible.

My Faith

Way deep down in the depths of the slums

I've been held as low as one man could ever go

I have nothing to show

Only thoughts of being a failure

Hoping for better ideals of how to merge into a better future

All that's left is my pride

Not letting my miseries keep me down

While still I'm aware that I can't do it alone

There is this saying, "nothing in life is for free"

As opposed to the word of God, it's free an a necessity

I'd over looked and pushed aside, knowing nothing about Him

Ashamed of the way I have lived

I fault myself for trusting Satan

I couldn't witness to it if I hadn't gone through it

I've overcome such catastrophe

And it happened all because I had faith

While trying to make a definite move and get my life back on track,
I still possessed burden tracks that lay deep on my heart.
Unselfishly thinking, I must return to that love which was true to
me.

Sorry

With my deepest concern and apology

I could not stay, you know I had to go

Pleasure got to know me by surprise

Tears of joy, I cry pain in the heart

I've been stabbed before

No, it did not change me

You were that thin line of love

What I've done might build hate

Leave your door opened wide

I must return with apology

Love just find it's own way

Times were unable to explain

Feelings just took right over me

Left such cold and lonely place

How can I forever concentrate

How can I accept my mistake

Now I am bleeding so very bad

All of my bleedings internally

True love is true and will not break

True love will return back to you safe

No one is perfect but make mistakes

Baby you know that, "I'm Sorry"

A moment of beauty, trust, care and concern, never did she change, she'd seem the same to me. Supposing I was right about the love of my life, or maybe for once, I had done something right. I'd become optimistic of her and saw the bigger picture once again.

Deja Vu

Sparkling eyes

I've seen that look before

The nourished

Thy supplier, is what she'd be

A mental conception of enhancement

I'm fed nutritiously

I nominate my sweet gorgeous

Thus, you're judged separately

Expressing my gratitude

I'm thankful for what you do

You're my Grand... My all

You're the Majestic one

Cool sensational clouds dilute heat from the sun

Rest assure be thy angel

Seems love been here before

I was fortunate during those times because I worked several jobs, still trying to locate me; instead did something. Giving many opportunities, if dissatisfied; I could always find employment someplace else.

Sweet USA

Working hard

No, I'm hardly working

The weatherman says it's going to rain

Five minutes late to my place of duty

Tomorrow search for another job

Never again will I miss thirty minutes of sleep

The mailman is running late

Maybe he's lazy too

The next day, as we stand in the same line

Applying for the same job

I love America

It is truly home of the free

Finally, I had drawn a conclusion; I'd decided to commit a few years and was willing to serve my country. This was not to separate from the one that I love; only an opportunity to be productive, the intent was never permanently.

Sweet Emotions

Skeptical thoughts intertwine

I draw visualized pictures with my mind

As if in a spade game

I try not to renege with you on my side

The price to pay isn't worth the lost

I refuse to cheat at any cost

My heart anticipates when your love is passed

I desire eternity with you

Our love is far above inseparable

I despise whispers from any hater mouth

Knowing their intensions is to interfere

You are forever the queen within my life

Who's forgiven already for no one is perfect

Fascinating is an expression of my love for you

Knowing not a single word is description of how I really feel

Therefore, if ever departing one another's sight

I fight time and not distance

My love will always be close to you

At this point of my life, I was missing my sweetheart, spending many nights alone; looked at stars with my pen and my pad. True enough she were my thoughts and that one to inspire me.

You

Beyond the galaxies of zodiac images

I thrust upon stars to seek love; obtruding unsolicited

Conspiracy thoughts, revolved mind of constellations

More than diamonds, star shinning so bright

Conception in particular, I direct my most attention

Mental faculty stimulated by such image

Depraved affections and a fond attachment

Behold an Angel in my regional stratosphere

I surface the entire globe to mold your space

Granted the years I've lived

Wishing to sustain the rest with you

My quantity of time is unknown but set limited

I thirst for more oxygen

Without you I can't breathe

I've realized the loneliness and emptiness of my legacy

Finding what's needed to fulfill my space

I'm filled up with you

Things started to look up and life seemed just a little bit better. I was having the time of my life without part two of me. Deep in my heart, I always knew that she'd feel the same. If there were any lost moments I didn't admit how I felt; I'd apologize, she should know love remains.

True Character of My Everyday Allusion

I really care for you

You never admit the same to me

I would do anything for you

Am I not worth listening to?

There are times when I want to just hold you

I catch a burning desire thinking of this love anticipation

A weird scenario is what it is

Can intoxication speak the truth?

I would give anything to know how you feel

I can't stop wondering if this feeling is real

I catch goose bumps when you're by my side

I'm always speechless when you look at me and smile

I tell myself, you have to know that I care for you

You never respond

Are you too shy, yet, feeling the same?

One last chance, if ever we're alone

Maybe I'll ask you

Please don't disappoint my heart

Just so you know

You really are the true character of my allusion

A more interesting part of my career starts to take place, I was being sent on a peacekeeping mission overseas to endure freedom. Distance takes toil on relationships; unintentionally neglect, all I had was proposing trust to get married.

Fiancé

So beautiful you are my brown eye princess

How bless you are to be so gorgeous

Your smile intrigue my most common thought

You take the place of that star, which lies in the north

I get lost in time reminiscing about you

Picturing possibilities seeing a great work of art

No, I'm not asleep, for I know that this is real

I provide my all to maintain your happiness

This is why I make the smaller things count

Such lonely place without appearance of your pretty eyes

Quite mysterious it get so cold out here in the sand

Not some place I wish to be, engaging at my enemies

It would be romantic if I could bring you to this place

Miles and miles so far away, still, you remain at heart

I stand alone in a different environment, being surrounded by such
huge mountains

I try and lace you with the most precious gift one could offer

I surrender my love, and devotion towards our relationship

Out of every dark cloud that's able to stop the sun from shining

There isn't a cloud dark enough to stop the shine you bring into my life

I contemplate occasionally what it's like to be committed

Until that time comes, I'll just call you my "Fiancé"

Writing had become one of my most desired hobbies. I had so little time to think, but so much to think about. Every day, I began writing in my journal; fascinated by the thoughts in my head.

Thoughts

Ι τραϖελ αλονε
I travel alone
Ι ωατχη πεολε
I watch people
Ι κεεπ το μψσελφ
I keep to myself
Ι φοχυσ βεττερ
I focus well

Ι ωριτε αλλ τηε τιμε
I write all the time
Ι ωριτε αβουτ οτηερσ
I write about others
Ι ωριτε ωηατ I φεελ
I write what I feel
Ι ωριτε το μαινταιν
I write to maintain

Ι τηινκ αβουτ λιφε
I think about life
Ι τηινκ αβουτ ψου
I think about you
Ι τηινκ τοο μυχη
I think too much
Ι τηινκ τηατ Ιэμ ριγητ
I think that I'm right

Ι δο ωηατ Ι χαν
  I do what I can
    Ι ηελπ οτηερ πεοπλε
      I help other people
        Ι δο ωηατ Ι φεελ
          I do what I feel
            Ι δο φυστ βεχαυσε
              I do just because

Ι κνοω ωηατ ιэμ σαψινγ
  I know what I'm saying
    Ι υνδερστανδ ωηατ Ι μεαν
      I understand what I mean
        Ι κνοω τοο μυχη
          I know too much
            Ι χανэτ στοπ τηινκινγ
              I can't stop thinking

Passionate thoughts I'd possess about my love, destined to be in her presence and around her existence. Expensive phone bill, we'd talk all the time; sharing those moments of how we wished it to be. Confined to the third degree, many nights we could not sleep, wishing for that moment we could breathe in and exhale.

Relief

Abstract art

My impulsive instinct can sense your silky element

Verbal cues of sexual exploits manipulate nature with vibrant pores

I explore within the wound, flesh, and beloved sensation

Perspiring much, driving deeper than any virtue to have ever dwelt

Breathing thick and heavily

I could hear your soul speak

Escaping your body as we dripped love

Free of mind with highlights of every touch

Restless hearts and despair of seduction

Indulgent and contrary to the way we both wish to feel

I'm happy now, I've received the greatest news; I was soon to be a proud father. If this didn't add spice to my life, then nothing would've. Telling the world, I've help create that special part of me.

Devotion

One sweet arousing moment intrigued us to intercourse

A lifetime invitation of me is what's left within you

Several months pass, now exists twice your beauty in disguise

The most precious gift that one could offer another

Hopes up high, experiencing new things in life

Important I be there, as she first touch ground into this world

Staring at her eyes, as my mind began to wonder

I'm a statue for life because she's my treasure

A love affair is what I've help to create

It will not
be easy, not to be so over protective

Let's hold hands my love, while I say this special prayer

In the end I'll be there, even if the Lord takes me away

Every now and then I'd relate with old friends I grew up with. We'd reminisce about incredible moments or simply life as teenagers. Those were the days and sometimes I really wish I could go back.

Times Sake

A cold world

Iceberg thoughts… the medulla has frozen

Still limping without a cane

Inner strength help to see the dead Eagle fly

He'd play his song

Peopled tip if they like… Hat to the side

Desperate he was

That ole box sounding better than a drum

Still so young… can't wait till I get grown

Thirsty for more

Sweaty years with a salty forehead

Shirt was off, I knew the game, I was truly good at it

Filling up my glass with another round of twenty-one

You lose you go home

Stream door wide open… Mama would always yell

Scrapping for change in her purse

Holidays were good if Papa played the right songs

Carrying the beats shoulder high

Ten plus size batteries to get it going

I'm no guru, but I knew what to do to keep a charge

Cardboard underneath... never direct concrete

Cutting filaments from various heads

Having skills and no license

I've become much older now, Hide and go Seek I use to play

Sometimes searching my younger days

Reminiscing for old times sake

Time moves on, but it seemed life had been stuck at a standstill; I was hoping to advance into the family life. What does it take to build a successful family? To be honest, all this time we've done our own carpentry.

Blue Print

The formality of love is designed by honesty and integrity

Each defined piece of the heart is structured by commitment

Guidance that provides a divine inspiration

Mental stability helping to create such great dynasty

It is a strategy of art to select the appropriate flesh

A concise biological sketch

Viewed and outlined with that of beauty

Every segment is so perfect made of the finest qualities

Desirable by choice when constructing a fabulous home

How essential it is to empower my every space

Voltage of love flows smooth, every vibe creating friction

Abstract meanings

Though my mind sense what it take to be happy

It is you I need most to help make my life complete

Just yesterday, I was thinking about having a family. Today, I have what I've always dreamed, my very own. That wife of mines is truly something; everyone says that we were meant to be together. Despite our ways as I know them to be different, I love that woman; she's the best part of me.

Wife

Wild hair... she sleeps so good

Up in the morning, still no change

Beautifully made exempting make-up

She makes up the bed, but still my cover girl

She'd wear my clothes; mines or hers didn't matter

I bought that shirt years ago, years ago I met her

Basketball was she and I favorite sport

Opposite teams in junior high, she'd talk about me

Calling me names like "e-walk," that was her favorite saying

She couldn't have said that... now she like me too much

High school were the days; she starts caring about me

Either she was just physic; yelp, she said we'd be together

Do you take this woman? I did, now she's in my life

Plain and simple she is as my dear and loving Wife

Here I am thinking again. Many times I just want to ease my mind and relax. Writing in comfort brings about my most intimate moments. Peacefully I am because my mind takes me there.

Imagine That

Imagine this, imagine that

What if you couldn't imagine?

Oh, then you couldn't see that

Gone like the wind…wild I am

The venturous one, imagining my own world

My planet's right here where everything seems great

With my pen and my pad, I can imagine what I want

The ocean's so beautiful with the rainbow in the back

Sounds of jazz music playing, who wouldn't want to imagine that?

I'm going to drink this wine on crushed ice and just chill

Enjoy my massage because that's how I feel

Run but don't stop, dare to get caught by waves

Those waves may take me back and I don't want to imagine that

I'm happy being married to a wonderful lady I can trust. She's truly my queen and deserves to be treated as such. For her, I'd be that perfect gentleman she desire; indeed, I'm the man for the job to always keep her happy.

Nubian Goddess

How great thou art to be your servant

So please I am considered your, I kiss your hand

Quite noticeable your beauty

No effort on your part

For I know not what you do to me

Your satin tone and silky blend

I present a red rose for such delightful appeal

Fashionable posture

You stand out amongst those not genuinely real

I pity the rest

Your fine self with a look that kill

Respectfully, I'm on call at your demand

Without unusual circumstance

I just know when my baby is in need

I write to vibes that is played at mellow tone. Saxophone blown and the tempo sound so grown. Me and myself I pour a tempting glass of wine, just patient ness I listen to my favorite song. Rhythm makes me and it also helps me think, cherishing the moments, I'll always appreciate.

Music

Can I elaborate?

This comprehensive statement I must make

Unfortunately, I have your attention

Soothing your flaws, I just might have the answer

Adhere to this, the way you feel I can relate

I challenge your mood by asking you on a date

You soul search, my capabilities can touch that too

I never asked to be a player, though it is what makes me

It's best I stay single too many people love me

You have a nice voice, ever been told you could sing?

Think I've found love; yes of course, we'd be the perfect match

Until death do us part, I'd never quit on you

Through blessings of the Lord I'm your gift to be given

Sunshine or cloudy days I will uplift your spirit

Emotional times of embarrassment; you don't care to explain

Hear me out a minute or two; I can make you smile again

I can be any way you wish me to be

Please hear what I say,

But you can't hear me until you've pressed play

... And that's Music

Throughout my career I've taken part in several deployments;
there's no greater joy than to finally return home.

The Flight

Standing in alphabetical order with dog tags hanging, identification cards at hand

Patiently waiting to be verified that you are that someone

Tired from such long day, energized from thoughts of happiness

You're about to head back home on the Great Big Bird

Wait! Screams out a commander, "were going to need a baggage detail"

Luckily you are to be an enlisted member; you just had to get chosen

Buses show up, you appreciate the ride to big bird land

Wow! Thrust with energy because that time has finally come

All aboard as everyone march like a pile of ants

Proceeding the steps being secured with high value dollar items

"Get in and sit down," applies a flight attendant

Quite difficult and very uncomfortable with all gear in your possession

Several minutes pass as rearrangement of personnel take place

"It's about time you may say," because now you're more relaxed

After all instruction regarding safety, you smile with head back,
chin pointed high up towards the ceiling

So comfortable, you doze off in only a matter of seconds

As the plane takes off you're in deep thought of heading home

In an hour you're awaken by the fresh smell of aroma

How thoughtful of the attendants to serve a meal

Delicious it was, again continuing your dream

The plane lands as you've reached your final destination

Saying, "I know that I'll be doing this again"

Since September 11th, the terrorist threat has been at an all time high, but We the People stand United and continue to move forward as trained professionals.

Spying Eye

The dark central opening of the iris

Kept open for reasoning of suspicion

A tear could blurry the vision

The physical sensation of perception

An insight of comprehension with a peripheral that can
acknowledge from both angles

The description is kept secret while glimpsing to speculate

Totally focused within reason, trained in guerilla warfare

Super vision, which can shadowbox with the enemy's intent

Like optical instruments zooming in from a far

The anticipation appears deadly

Camouflaging one's self to foresee any suspicious act

The mission prolongs, while trying to receive data

Wearing a white shirt and tie, undercover as the investigator

A great moment in life makes it easy to appreciate Faith. For so long I've been guilty at conscious wondering what shall I do? As a soldier in the United States Army, it doesn't become easier to live the right life. Of course there's protocol, but that's with every job. I find peace within myself by conversation with God, for I'm sure that He will always listen.

Soul Presentation

Here I am Lord wearing all this camouflage

Carrying a rucksack with all the pieces of my life

The sack was a little torn

I lost some pieces along the way

I hope they were not the good ones

Then of course, I'd have to explain

Sorry for dirty boots

I got them dirty during the war

I know… I know… I had them on during those times of sin

Please understand, I was only doing my job

I've become wiser and realize that particular job's not for me

During the election, I only voted for you Lord

Your home is the only place that I wish to deploy

That is, I've been properly trained to serve you

My trust is with you, thus, the nation lies too

On my knees I pray that I manifest through your gate

I surrender my life, though that wouldn't be enough

You're the true Commander, the only one I'd salute

And oh Lord… those pieces that I lost were good deeds from the heart

There's a much greater love than people know. Love sits on high;
love is true and love is not afraid to show. How true must one be to
love another? I'm destined to know, although I say I love my own.
Many people of the world use the word love in vain.

True Love

It's clear to me what love really mean

With an exception of sin, love is purification meaning clean

For Him I shall strive sharing His words with many others

Faithfulness is mandatory, definitely sisters and brothers

How could we stand this moment Lord, hadn't it been for you?

You're the necessity we need most in order for us to pursue

Many days appear hard while the nights last so long

With Him lies my destiny motivating me to drive on

I encourage the weaker ones, like myself a time before

Isolation from a sinful nature is the direction to so much more

For who shall I neglect when I'm suppose to help them

I can assure that I've been blessed because someone told me of Him

Like a fugitive I've chose to run away to escape from that of evil

Thank you Lord for a second chance to associate with better people

Like gold are the words that He speak, without a price He leaves to receive

It's your option to invite Him into your life, for the option is yours to believe

While reading these words does it boost you morale, or not mean a thing?

Remember He died on the Cross for our sins, took punishment being serious abused

Now that's "True Love"

Stranded on a desert island in the middle of nowhere; a moment like this makes it easier to appreciate everything. Unsure if I would make it home safe, always on my guard, I sit still; so many thoughts in my head. Being far away, help me to realize the love I have was so special. I must find a way to communicate; she must know that I love her too.

A Bottled Message

Never have I endured so much pain

I crater my own life keeping myself safe for you

Pain is devastating without an issue of unperceived medicine

No one knows but you and I

Frustration of love that lies behind the intimate walls

All the writing on the walls, the fine lines that are written

Carved and engraved with our names so we'd see

I pity my life without you I've truly fallen

You mean the world to me, my right hand that I need

You'd go that extra mile not concerned that it's green

This genuine heart of loneliness painted thin

Those times of dishonesty, I regret when it rained

A made love, so profound and insane

I knew nothing about what the Lord had in store

You stood before me, reeled me in with enchantment

Such hot and tempting flame, so hot we'd make steam

Yet, cooled off from life reality… Icebergs

I've touched your heart, the same rhythm as mines

When I'm awake and can't sleep I'd know that you're pacing

Enormous size heart that encounter so much pain

Possessing eager moments with no longer a massage

I'd die to ignite that old candle once lit

While returning to you without a reasonable doubt

True love still exist in the mind of imagination

Touching the untouchable of that I can not see

I've witness true love it was once given to me

This love will not end if true love's meant to be

This message for you, I'll assume it'll reach

From your soul mate, placed in a bottle along the shore

As time progressed, thoughts about going home became immeasurable. No one wants to feel unworthy of his or her being, I only wanted to express my gratitude and show appreciation for the things that she did. For so long and so much of the time, I'd think of my love and the type of husband I need to be.

Casual Thoughts

I've thought before but never like this

My mind has reached its maximum capacity of thoughts about you

Sometimes is never the case, but all the time for sure

Patiently, my concern stands strong on your behalf

A disturbed mind, what makes me feel the way I feel?

When I feel this way, I still feel so not real

As time passes me, it kills me

Excluded from your every space of expectancy

I long for your companionship as a lover and friend

Proceeded by wishes, derived from blessings and never the
impossible

I hold the same flame as before

Getting nowhere, devastated over the time we've been together

Imagination makes life

Many things said may be a lie, because the mind is unable to speak
for itself

I balance my imagination to analyze with wise words being spoken

Now you have just heard the truth

I really appreciate everything you've done for me

Don't ever change being special

I love you the way you are

With every marriage comes a discrepancy. I faced my times as they really changed me. I was a bad reflection of the mirror with myself standing in it. I had to become mature, wake up or lose everything I'd own.

Change

The perpetual spirit of an annoying image

An act of unceasing continuing forever

The soul tends to ache when the heart impersonates

Pretending to be a character showing selflessness that's unacceptable

Like a sharp sworn object slowly slicing the better half

Taking advantage in such ways, while true love is make belief

Announcing the thrown of eternal love

Partaking in a ceremony of Holy matrimony

Peculiar traits disguised by the devil himself

The heart beats for reasoning

Pulsation drawn by rhythmic contractions

In the art for which insufficient love is dispensed

May cause grief or extreme hurt of distress

This cause for a Change

Many times, understanding what I could've lost, forced me to soul search for the unknown credits of how to strengthen that relationship. It was like trying something new; yet different, all those things I should've done in the first place. I'll never ever stoop so low, not ever again.

Alcoholic

The Liquid sword touches my tongue with a chase

Left with a frown from a spark of lemon twist

I thirst for the unknown of conspicuous drink

Bottle so ancient… Rum made in Great Britain

Highly impaired, a morbid affect to the stomach

Regretting those times, when I wanted to have had

Internally traumatized, wishing I didn't drink

Perspiring much from my pores and lacking water

Incision was sharp… cutting me deep into a sleep

Awaken was I, diagnosis to a fem.

Make up or breakup, I definitely had to get it together. It was never materialistic things that mattered, but all those things the size of a grain of salt. I'd miss my love, and I'm sure she wished for the old me back. She was spoiled and I had changed from being me. I was better than that just had to prove her so.

Now that's Destiny

I know what it's like to feel insignificant

Circumstances stand outside your control

Intrigued by all of the smaller things

Never have you been treated like this before

No explanations as problems stand undefined

Quiet walks in the park to try and wonder why

The sincerity of that person shows how much they care

Therefore, you fall in love with the person of your dreams

A distinctive individual is who they are

A distinguished Angel is what they appear to be

Wishing the heart speak a language that you understand

To tell you love like this doesn't fade momentarily

It's not a moment everyday you don't think of that someone

Reckless and determined, desperate you are to be with them

They are your designated request upon arrival

You crave with lust and aspiration they were near

You desert most of your energy trying to keep yourself together

In this case, time doesn't fulfill its obligation

Patiently, it seems you'll be waiting forever

Hoping and wishing love would find its way home

Needless to say, my old lady was more than a woman to me. She did her part and sometimes mines too. Any fool wouldn't recognize such a beautiful thing. I knew what I had and wouldn't risk losing her for anything. She's every man dream, but she was all mines.

Brown Sugar

Simply irresistible

I am but a magnet just to your smell

Your physical appearance ultimately disables my deliberate act

No accusations, just heartbeat pacing

Who is number one stunting?

Of course you are

You ignite me

No home remedy can cure this status paralysis

Your beauty is lethal with a breathtaking fate

Everyone knows that's not legal

My sweet tooth for your candy I am willing to get a cavity for

Persuasive by inspiration, with no discussions, or any misconceptions

You hold down your own for sure

I can't give you up and that's what's up

Never pulling my wisdom tooth, because I'm sure you're the one

I'm appreciative of beautiful days that the Lord so bless the world to have. Again, with my pen and my pad, I'd write while acknowledging natures finest. I'm sure they appreciate such lovely days too. I was bored, but lazy anyhow.

Mocking Bird

A puddle of water

Watching birds soak their feet while the ambient temperature
remain so high

Sipping lemonade

Love Serenade

I listen to… sung by Barry white

From an old juke box

Stored down stairs in my Grandfather's basement

Cobb webs, this place is filthy

I help Mama clean up

So hungry I'm starving

I can't wait to eat

I must first bathe like the birds, then feed them crackers

For it was them which inspired me

Well, here I am leaving one military post off to the next. I was certain not to deploy anytime soon, but that's not necessary true. Perhaps, I was chosen to depart the family again, I was sure to be worry free and that my wife would wait for me. If it were she, I'd do the same for her.

Patience

I'd wait for you until my blood runs thin

Every second is crucial as I hear the clock tick.

Changing weather, still I remain on that bench

The bench we sat on and the place we first met

Never asking for much, only time does not stop

Cause then it'll be longer until I see you again

People wonder by laughing and calling me a fool

Who cares what they think? This is I needing you

Over the years I've seen much, except your return

Old and Grey I still wait, for your love I've earned

Crash Course

Who's talking?

Who's listening?

Why and what is really the ordeal?

I miss your point; I had something to say too

Every news spokesman speaks relatively of the same old sad things

Who's talking?

Who's listening?

Why and what is really the ordeal?

Who's talking? We are

Who's listening? They are

Why and what is really the ordeal?

Too much information about us is a tribute for planning their next attack

Who's talking?

Who's listening?

Why and what is really the ordeal?

Let's take more time to acknowledge those individuals who may be listening to us, then maybe we can help do away with the killings of our own kind

If you're talking, maybe you should listen

"That is really the Ordeal"

Back on the basketball court again, just to see if I still had it.
Obviously, I had been pre-selected to be an All Army basketballs
participate. Things didn't happen as I imagined due to injury. I
returned back home, now giving props to younger generation.

Destiny's Dream

Dream any longer

Never could I admit to myself that it's over

By a freight train, I've been hit once too many times

I'm not the same ole me anymore

Yes, I could still do it

Never would I admit to myself that it's over

A tear falls from the eye, I've become an instructor

Reminiscing of past times, it was me that use to shine

I'm a changed man, yet, to experience new things in life

Never could I admit to myself that it's over

Migraine headaches, tossing and turning trying to sleep

I've realized I can't make the same moves anymore

Never could I admit to myself that it's over

I've lost my fan club, guessing things happen for a reason

Still, never will I admit to myself that it's over

I miss those days of getting my props on the basketball court. Now I focus more on staying in shape, keeping toned with my Physique. I don't normally give myself credit for anything, but just as the average individual, we all have our days of being conceited.

Crush

I exist in the form of appraisal

Anatomy for seduction

Mouth watery, drooling

Appetite for love is so overruling

The quench of thirst, goose bumps

Perspiration like the opening of a sprite

Pleased with results in the mirror

Standing posed, handsome

Choosing self for nominations award

Such curves in the abdominal

No sign of speed bumps to stop me now

Critical I say, but I tell you more

A foundation is made with an ultimate touch

Being placed here so that beauty wouldn't want to let go

Feeling good-looking good, I was sure to ask the wife out on a date.
It's always nice to share a lovely occasion with the one you love.
That night, I had thoughts of becoming intoxicated without the
alcohol. I knew she'd love me for that.

Propose a Toast

I would like to propose a toast to an undying love

Admirable she is, wine glasses touch

Such fine tune like a key from the piano

Exchange of arms, we sipped from each others wine glass

My deepest thoughts, she thinks too

Just the two of us enjoying such lovely occasion

"May I have the, from her lips, I am asked to dance"

Mellowed and soothing, the arena of love

Expiring limitations, as we dance on and on

Gently by the hand, holding her ever so tightly

Silly intoxications, as I spend her around and around

Today is our day tomorrow hope the same

A heartfelt moment with no intensions of letting go

After a nice and lovely evening, most times, there is icing to put on a cake. Neither my wife nor I spoke Spanish, sending vibes to each other, as if we both spoke another language. We are familiar with another language that all races are capable of recognizing.

Second Language

I sense a casual speech that's peculiar to yours

Your general style of expression says more than just hello

Body interpretations surrender a transalpine vibe

Loving the way you use your tongue to make words sound like that

Pronunciation seem to be my frustration

Hard, yet difficult, to express what I feel

Honey dip, your sweet fingertip licking

So sticky I'm tripping

Captivating to that mode of sexual healing

The look, the touch, and the feel

I'm forced to take you there

The circumference of your space, lateral space, everywhere

I want to sing to you, my songs different this time

Keeping the tone at low volume, just enough to wet the ear

No games for real, now you now that I'm for real

What are my chances with you?

Now is your chance to be with me

You lick your lips to keep my mind manipulated

I watch those hips, imagining thighs marinated

Candles go out, wax get poured in the right spots

Loving the hot sensational touch a whole lot

Not knowing what's being said, but understanding body tainting

I can honestly say it certifies as my official Second Language

Everyone wonders how my marriage sustains the test of time. Well, it's a fifty-fifty love and both have to understand and compromise. I knew what to expect before being introduced to marriage, I learned from everyone else's' mistakes. Anytime you find someone who would go that extra mile, not being concerned that it's green, they are probably worth keeping. Let the truth be told, it's difficult to find a Diamond in the Rough.

Diamond in the Rough

You are my Diamond in the Rough

My statue of liberty stands tall with you

While in that three point stand

So erotic, I'm hypnotic just by starring at you

My desire for you is an objective with a high altitude

Not to exclude you in any way, but to treat you exclusive

Sweet like music, you run laps around my mind

Intercept my thoughts like an eclipse

Drifting off in the outer limits of ecstasy

The idea is to keep you mine

We both drink a little wine

Without intoxication, everything about you still remain the same

You bruise me

I'd give everything if I had everything

I love you

Must I say, you're all that and then some too?

The mood is passionate without candles

Moon providing our guiding light

You look exquisite when the light hits your tone

My tongue marathon the juices of your every sweet portion

I think of you all the time, not just some of the time

The way I fault in this war

Who'd think it was about you and not Saddam

Statistics phenomenal, I've dealt with the toughest times

Loosing no composure while trying to keep, my diamond in the rough

My marriage isn't perfect, but it is something special. Most couples experience divorces, simply, because they didn't try hard enough. I was always sure that my wife wouldn't say no when proposing to her. I was also sure that she needed me, as much as I needed her. For anyone who's unsure about his or her other half use patience to understand his or her mood indigo.

Mood Indigo

I stand here proposing to you

So cold with rejection... should you treat me this way?

Celsius twenty below total embarrassment

I shed no tear, but still everyone was looking

Returned myself in the opposite direction

Direction to which, I first purchased the ring

My heart's now pale, stale, deprived of joy

First time on me, second... shame on you

Unusual reasoning kept my heart beating fast

Pulse at maximum pace, dare you treat me this way

Your treacherous heart couldn't except the fate

Denying my love; reconstructing in a subsidiary way

This plant has died, you couldn't change a thing

Regretting that moment I met your Personality

Many times in life things happen for no apparent reason, or are there reasons; the mind has yet, to accept? I had foreseen myself as a potion being mixed, unintentionally; I am an ingredient of self-taught with a thirst for knowledge and understanding. I am who I am today, what I've learned and know is what makes me what I am.

Formula

A child is born with no intentions on purpose

Triggered thoughts of having knowledge

In my veins flows wisdom to know it all

Life potion being designed with confusion

Schematics of a genius, I teach myself to understand

What is real, ever so genuine, and of truth, this I wonder?

Life offerings seem distant to those appearing helpless

Front cover of the world, publicizing before the media

I enhance my thoughts composing mixtures of intelligence

Political views, brainwashed methods and raw teachings

I was never created from such chemical composition

An influence, a positive me, eyes opened to the world

Strategic thoughts and ideas dosed of abstract medicine

A blood stream of inner strength, to breathe and live, I exist

A seminal fluid made typically whole

Once part solution, until that very day I was conceived

In the world today, many people require attitude adjustments. These people are impatient and want everything to happen all at once. When things don't go their way they overreact. These individuals aren't crazy, they lack psychological assistance. I have always understood people for how they are, and because I have, it's been easy to understand their personality. This way, I can continue to be common in mind.

Something Else

A walking time bomb

A mind of frustration with a spark

A detonating pause in which time will reveal

Decrepit mood of deranged affects

Disorderly functions isolated with no sense of reality

Pressured fuse blown from a mishap reasoning

Stay away, at this moment, it's best to be alone

Tangled thoughts, blood runs backward in the mind

Impeding slower with a vision to retaining memory

Disembodiment of self which appears unnatural

Disbanding functions that are ill and disturbed

Dislocated skull beholds a nervous sensation

Illiteracy deception, ill tempered with a rehab negligence

The world is fulfilled with many people of such character

Lack psychological help; attitudes are impatient

Yet, they're not crazy, these people are something else

Sometimes taking a risk can be an in creditable thing. Imagine if one never took a risk for anything; you'd never succeed or know the outcome of a successful attempt. While wanting something so badly, I never thought secondly about doing what I must to achieve my ultimate goal.

Chances

My Little Stallion

Very unique with style, she entice my entire momentum

I tremble at heart not to know how she thinks

But her style takes us right back to home

Look at you, a diamond stare I can't stop

So tempted I am, I've needed you for so long

I breathe anciently to see your face

Caressing my thoughts, this of course includes you

A diehard of feistiness, stimulating a sexy charge

Her reasoning for Cause and Effect

I could affect the way she feels forever

I want to be your passionate lover

I want to be your great escape

Needing you, but you needing me

We could be one, but understand that existing is two

Rain is such beautiful result poured on nature

Cage birds sings, like a baby we're both fast asleep

Drenched in chills, overcoming our fears

An incredible risk, with only one life to live

All the money in the world means nothing without love. Ask a rich
individual; so silly, to think any differently. I always felt it was
about money to keep a person happy, I was proven wrong, money
can't buy what we all desire most; love.

Subliminal

I wish to conquer your love without a trace

Surround our space of concrete walls so no one would interrupt

I'm submissive unto you because you're so great

A boomerang love with an affect that always keep me coming back

Despair of romance I often dream

Obtruding your love, I am persistent with disturbing your emotions

I feel so obligated to provide love of your indebt ness

I sense what you require, in test of time; love will prevail

Hold me ever so tightly; convince me you've lost the key

This is between you and me; for such long time, I could hardly wait

A distinct model of eloquence

A compound frame composed of drooling assemblies

Sweet love you're so fine, never could anyone take that away

Teach me how to obtain your perfect quench

An attic requiring love to endure this gratification

I sit here proposing myself a drink, allocations behind love; never caring about the heart in which I steal. Rudely imposed by depression, I drink heavily; obtaining no conclusion of what makes me feel this way. Happiness is from within the divine soul, I seek to know love; love is what helps me overcome being out of control.

Exploitation

I've circled the globe in one piece

Pieces of the heart, now shattered and spread amongst many of the world

Truly I've identified love; a selfish love

Unbalancing, emotional equilibrium

Companion was the ultimate demand

Leave me be, I'm left lonely with a reap what you sow

So sorry am I to play those games

It was all an act, portraying king, as if the true Messiah

With no opposing trust, I have danced and made love

A moment of disadvantage, tangled sheets and gone by morning

Articulate by nature, so sure you'd understand

I knew what to say; love is what I'd always given

It's such wonderful experience just to say what I've done

So sad but I don't regret taking my chances to explore

The most desirable eye candy is one who sparks another's attention by his or her enchanting eloquence. Often like a dream while I hope, I'd thirst for the one of the best

Elite

Hello gorgeous, you possess that I see

The best body, truly amazing with a stunting eloquence

Seems you have an advantage on my thoughts

Protecting your goods, rejecting pleasure to remain in your circle

In the eye of the beholder your heart lay

I understand now, but do not understand what's next for me to say

You stand out amongst those of feminine flesh

Your heart is of gold, splendid realism with a genuine affect

Feed me knowledge to gain infatuated approach

You laugh I smile back, while gaining a moment of optimism

Your intelligent self, short; stimulating mood of gratification

Paying attention to your vibes, listening to every word you say

Imagine living without the one you share most of your time with, imagine loneliness in despair of someone. To have someone on your side, more like another half; things are just so much better this way

Battle Buddy

Dear friend of mine

How nice of you to find the time

To share with, and be with only me

You said you have my back

Well, I got your back too

Acknowledging your soreness,

Massaging your legs, I would gladly do for you

The Fahrenheit in the room could have changed

Instead we stay calm, you were right I shouldn't drink

Extended work day, appearing awesome to hear your voice

I'll care for you much, always here when you need me

Our time may run short, let's enjoy while we can

N E way as you would say, because it is… what it is

We're Battle Buddy's!

To God Almighty for every day is your day. I send you praise and acknowledgment for just being kind to me. You offer me today and I accept it proudly; while this is my chance to be the head of my home.

Happy Fathers Day

Happy fathers day to every dad as you were created,

How important you are, a vital role called upon by Jesus Himself

You fulfill an ultimate role in this life time as a parent

If not to your own child, then maybe to someone else's

Look at you stand, head of house being tasked by God

Disregarding situations, for His blessings will allow you to do the best you can

The first ancestor, an early expounder of Christianity

I want to thank you Lord for making me special, and for blessing me with today

I speak on behalf of those fathers who aren't here

For it is still your day, you're with the Lord now and have already celebrated

You help me to stay calm, keep my cool and be collective

I realize today is special, so I except it with a smile

As you anoint my head with oil my cup runs over

I wish to spill your word Lord, for my goodness is surely your mercy

Many times things appear unbearable, but today it seems ok

Acknowledging you God with praise on this very particular day

Although today may reference all dads, Heavenly father it's still about you

You know I wouldn't be here this very moment and to speak

And for that I'd like to say, "Thank you"

To every father in this world, blessed you are to receive directives in Jesus name

Continue to smile with your chin pointed high

Once again, He has blessed us with another glorious day. Happy fathers day!

To my God, you are my father in control of the universe; I look to seek your face, for your smile makes me smile. Today I realize the truth; here I stand all because of your love and grace.

Heavenly Father

Heavenly Father, thou control of Heaven and earth

I'm submissive unto you because you're so great

While seeing the depths of how bad things could actually be

I rebuke Satan in your name, for He would never conquer me

Again and again you lift my soul entirely

I want to thank you Great Father for looking upon me and my family

Though you hear my shout, whether I'm rejoicing or while praying

For your name will be glorified through my praising you constantly

It is me my lonely self needing you so badly

My ultimate goal is to be where you are, for I know you'll take care
of me

Hear me cry out loud through conversations with you

Cross my heart with love that every word I say is true

As I speak to the crowd that sits before me today

Like a new born baby, I acknowledge you as my Lord and only
Savior

Ever wish to have the answers behind the importance of living? I thirst for Longevity, a piece of mind; time to interact with God. Humble I choose to be; alone at times, peacefully I utilize this time to find me.

Piece of Mind

My life is but a journey all along,

While traveling an extensive tour of the unknown to find destiny in some sacred place

I surrender my thoughts, placing me deep into a stare

Lying in the corner of the mind; a dark hole of frustration and built tension

Eternal spark, of what life is and to live

Resulting to this lifetime; still bleed fully ripe

With constant search, a winded tunnel of breathe in despair of oxygen

Lead me now into your palace, spark able remarkable Almighty one

For your word as it is written, your intelligent saber cuts me deep the way you speak

The smile of life from your face makes me smile

I perish so slowly without an honorary touch

Tonight I'll dream, praying before going to sleep

If I don't wake up, so sure you'll take me with you

About the Author

Terrance B. McGee, is a resident of Nolanville, Texas; an Equipment Set Specialist with Data Solutions and Technology. Along with writing, he finds essential continuation to support the troops, for he himself, served a faithful nine years in the United Army. Writing is his most desired passion, while his tenure in service contributed immeasurably to the expansion of his works. He is married with a family of four; family oriented, and loves spending time with his family. Besides that, he is fascinated with utilizing his creativity to create great works for many to read and to watch. His focus also, is to produce great works that are inspiring to all, as much as it was for him to write and create it. His study is Journalism, while he allows his creative writing skills to extend beyond his desire and motives. His passion is to become an indispensable poet throughout the field of writing, and spark interest of many throughout the world.

For ideal credits and comments, you may contact me at:
terrancemcgee27@yahoo.com or terrance.b.mcgee@us.army.mil

Printed in the United States
74590LV00004B/129